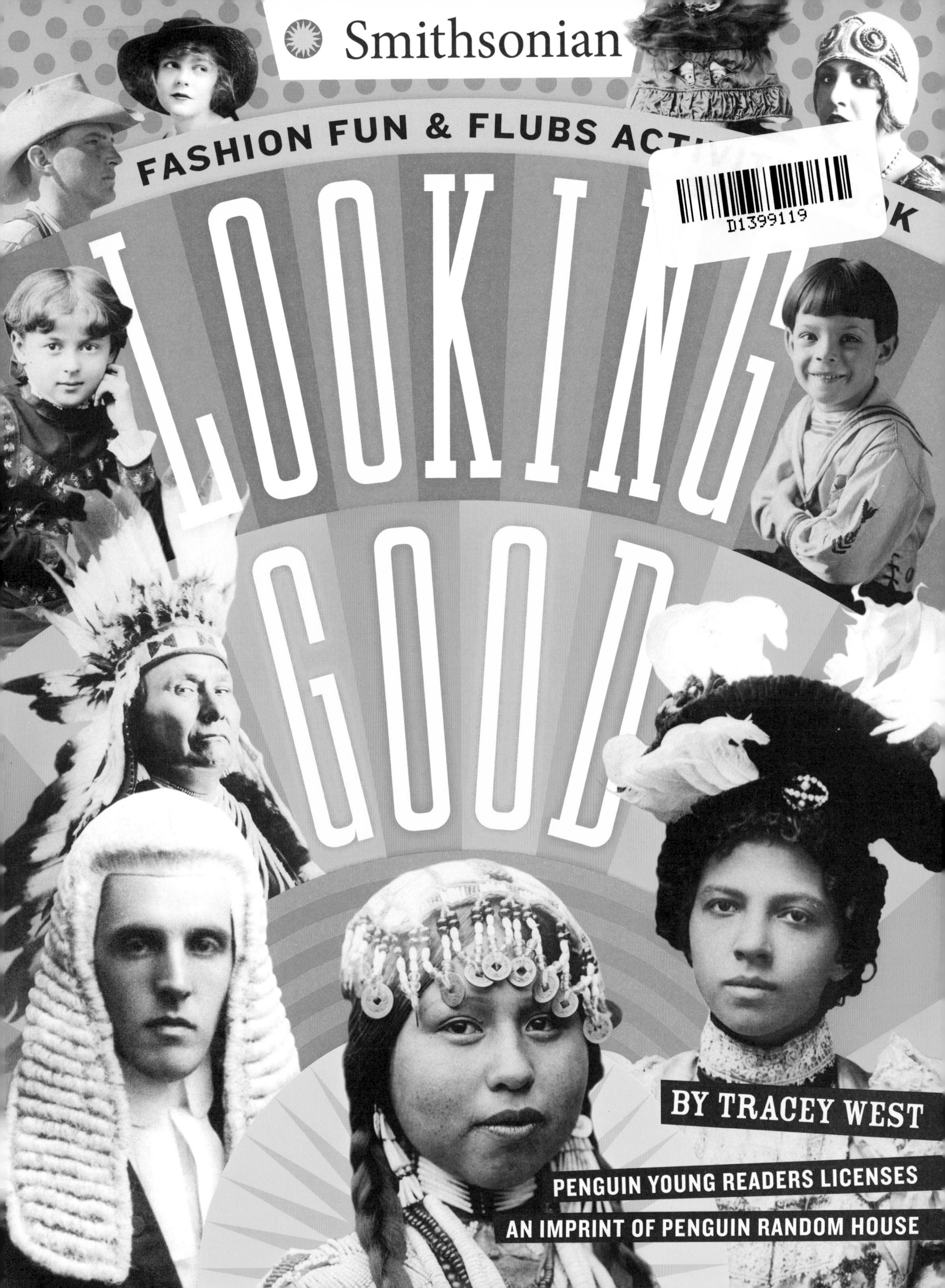
Smithsonian
FASHION FUN & FLUBS ACTI
OK
D1399119
LOOKING
GOOD
BY TRACEY WEST
PENGUIN YOUNG READERS LICENSES
AN IMPRINT OF PENGUIN RANDOM HOUSE

PENGUIN YOUNG READERS LICENSES
An Imprint of Penguin Random House LLC

PHOTO CREDITS

FLICKR: 9 (chokecherry, photo by Katja Schulz); 49 (top right, photo by shortiestar 3000); 50 (left, The National Archives UK); 61 (top right and bottom left, photos by David DeLeon/www.petful.com); 63 (cocktail dress, photo by Solarbotics).

JGB SERVICE: 6–7 (maze).

LIBRARY OF CONGRESS: front cover, 1 (all images); back cover (top row: cat, teen girl with big hat, man in aviator hat; second row: woman in tiara; third row; woman at bottom); 3; 10; 11 (cowboy boots, children stacking shoes); 12 (Wishram bride); 14 (wigs at top, man at bottom left, modern wig shop); 16 (top row, except bonnet at far right; second row, except top hat; third row, left and center; bottom row, except pink hat and man on far right); 17 (man at bottom right); 20 (center); 28 (both images); 40; 41; 42; 43; 46 (all images except top left); 56 (top left); 58 (bottom right); 60 (right); 61 (top left and bottom right); 64; stickers (cat, Wishram bride, boy, woman in curtain hat, wigs, flapper).

PATRICK SMITH: 60 (left).

SMITHSONIAN: back cover (suit of armor); 4 (all clothes); 8 (bottom left); 11 (grass shoes); 12 (blue hair ornament; Kuba belt); 16 (bonnet, top hat, beaded hat, pink hat); 18 (Indian woman); 20 (top right, bottom left); 25 (bottom left); 26–27 (all images); 30; 31; 32 (all images); 34 (two images of silkscreening in top right); 35 (kimonos at bottom); 39 (suit of armor at left); 44; 45; 46 (top left); 47 (all images except woman at top right); 56 (top right, bottom left and right); 58 (bottom left); stickers (top hat, beaded hat, pink hat, woman in sari, suit of armor, dresses, man in blue suit, belt, headdress, boots at bottom right).

THINKSTOCK: back cover (boy in baseball cap, photo by Digital Vision); 4 (raccoon, photo by GlobalP); 5 (photo by GlobalP); 6 (llama, photo by JackF; lamb, photo by GlobalP; two alpacas, photo by GlobalP; yarn, photo by oatll); 7 (sheep, photo by GlobalP; mittens, photo by taratata); 8 (mummy, photo by Photos.com); 9 (honey locust, photo by Tuned_In; mulberries, photo by ValentynVolkov; stinging nettles, photo by scisettialfio; acorns, photo by dionisvero; walnut shell, photo by johnandersonphoto; indigo, photo by yogesh_more); 11 (sneakers, photo by Jarretera); 16 (bottom row, far right, photo by Jupiterimages); 17 (hard hat, photo by structuresxx; cowboy hat, photo by brandysites; helmet, photo by abadonian; sombrero, photo by Riccardo_Mojana; visor, photo by praethip; cap, photo by kitthanes; tricorne, photo by WesAbrams; beret, photo by lepas2004); 18 (fabric, photo by miflippo); 34 (silkworms, photos by Kaan Sezer; scarf at bottom left, photo by ElenII; scarf at bottom center, photo by sergarck; scarf at bottom right, photo by Issaurinko); 36 (photo by Jupiterimages); 49 (poodle, photo by GlobalP); 50 (woman at top right, photo by iconogenic; tie-dye, photo by flukesamed); 52 (photo by Yuri Arcurs); 53 (left, photo by ginosphotos; center, photo by Digital Vision; right, photo by moodboard); 54 (photo by monkeybusinessimages); stickers (cap, photo by kitthanes; beret, photo by lepas2004; cowboy boots, photo by mattiestudio; sneakers, photo by Jarretera).

WIKIMEDIA COMMONS: 9 (alder bark, photo by Walter Siegmund; butternut shell, photo by Modal Jig); 12 (Hindu bride, photo by Nirmal Dulal); 14 (British court wigs, photo by Oxfordian Kissuth; Egyptian stone carving, photo by Walters Art Museum; King Louis XIII, public domain); 17 (chiton and toga, public domain); 22 (women in hoop skirts, public domain); 33 (Barack and Michelle Obama, public domain); 35 (top right, photo by Peabody Essex Museum); 38 (Joan of Arc, public domain); 39 (suit of armor at right, photo by Rama); 47 (top right, public domain); 48 (top right, public domain); 51 (left, photo by Mike Powell; right, photo by Daniel Hartwig).

Published by Penguin Young Readers Licenses, an imprint of Penguin Random House LLC, 345 Hudson Street, New York, New York 10014.
Manufactured in China.

ISBN 9780515159066 10 9 8 7 6 5 4 3 2 1

CONTENTS

MADE OF . . .

WORK IT!

When early humans needed clothing to stay warm or protect themselves from the elements, they worked with what they had: animals. Animal hides and fur could be draped, wrapped, or stitched. People sewed with tools made of bone and threaded with stringy animal tissue. Some American Indians mixed water and animal brains into a paste to tan hides, which made clothing softer.

CIRCLE THE NAMES OF 14 ANIMALS THAT HUMANS HAVE USED TO MAKE CLOTHING. SEARCH UP, DOWN, ACROSS, BACKWARD, AND DIAGONALLY.

D	L	B	E	A	V	E	R	I
E	O	U	N	T	X	I	G	E
E	R	F	L	O	W	B	E	L
R	A	F	F	R	L	K	L	E
M	I	A	T	I	B	B	A	R
P	O	L	A	R	B	E	A	R
H	T	O	M	M	A	M	O	I
N	T	T	S	I	R	A	C	U
S	E	A	L	E	E	Y	W	Q
E	R	A	C	C	O	O	N	S

DRAW A WOOLLY LINE TO SOMETHING WARM TO WEAR.

Human beings started raising sheep for food around 12,000 years ago. They also realized that if wool kept sheep warm, it could keep shepherds warm, too! A few thousand years later, people in Peru figured out how to use the fibers of llamas and alpacas to make clothing. First, spin the wool into thread or yarn. Then weave the yarn into cloth, and sew!

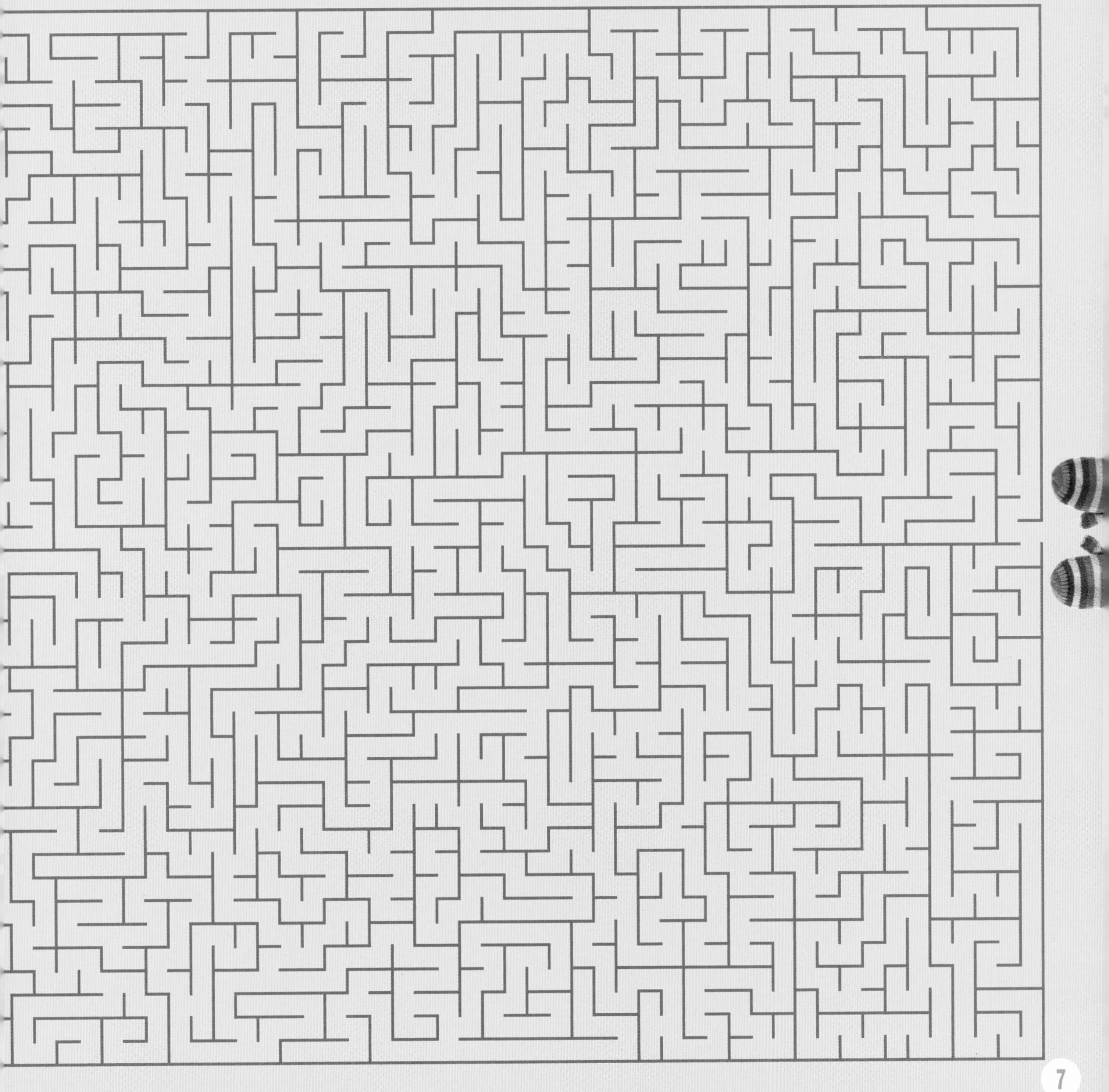

MADE OF . . .

GROW YOUR CLOTHES

At least 5,000 years ago, people spun thread from plants. Fluffy, white cotton was one of the first plant parts that was woven and worn. In ancient Egypt, the flax plant was used to make linen—for the living *and* the dead. Egyptians wore linen garments and wrapped mummies in the cloth.

Clothing got a lot more colorful in 2600 BCE when people started using plants to dye fabrics. Bark, berries, roots, leaves, or even entire plants were used to produce colors.

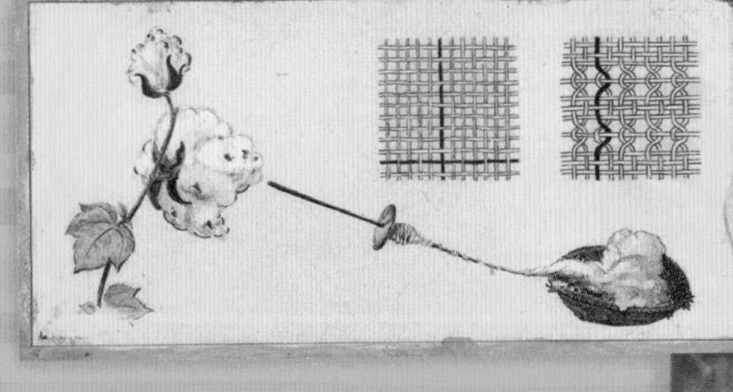

▲ a cotton boll

THESE NORTH AMERICAN PLANTS HAVE ALL BEEN USED TO MAKE CLOTHING DYES. DRAW A LINE FROM EACH PLANT TO THE COLOR IT COULD MAKE.

1 honey locust	A black
2 alder bark	B blue
3 chokecherry	C brown
4 mulberries	D gray
5 stinging nettle	E green
6 butternut shells	F orange
7 acorns	G purple
8 walnut shells	H red
9 indigo	I yellow

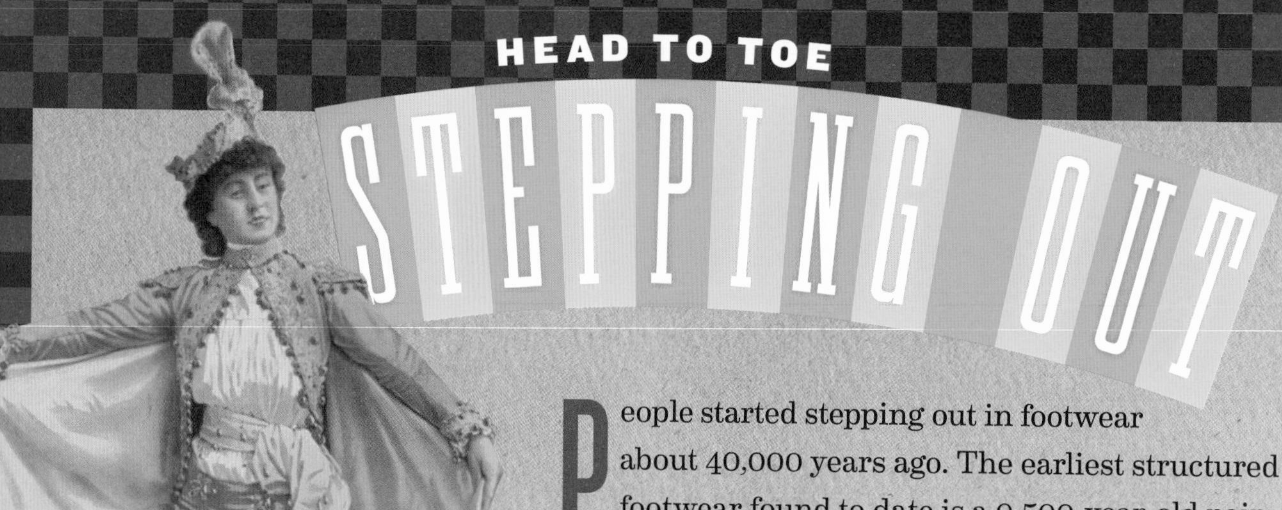

STEPPING OUT

People started stepping out in footwear about 40,000 years ago. The earliest structured footwear found to date is a 9,500-year-old pair of sandals made from the sagebrush plant. They were discovered in a cave in Oregon.

All kinds of materials have been used to make shoes: grass, bark, cloth, wood, and of course, the ever-popular leather. In the twentieth century, the list expanded to include synthetics. Check your soles or sneakers!

DESIGN A SHOE FOR EACH SEASON.

SPRING

SUMMER

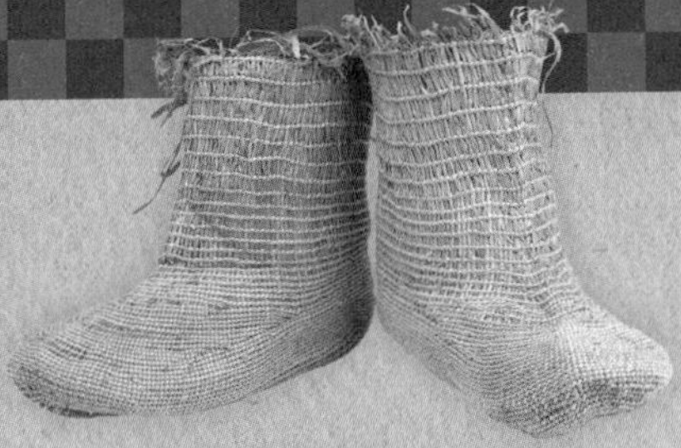

▲ grass, Aleutian Islands, Alaska

▼ leather, USA

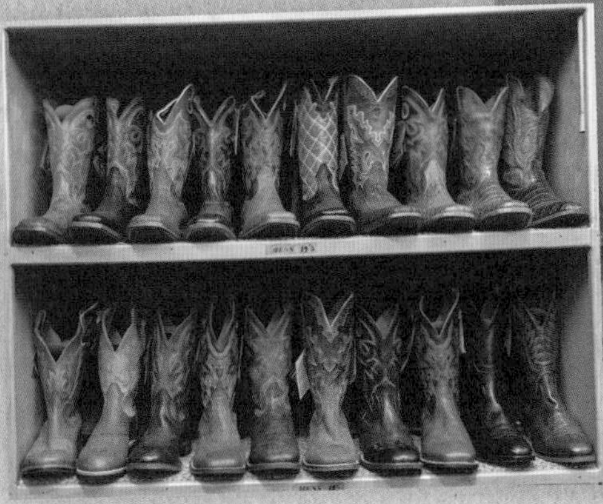

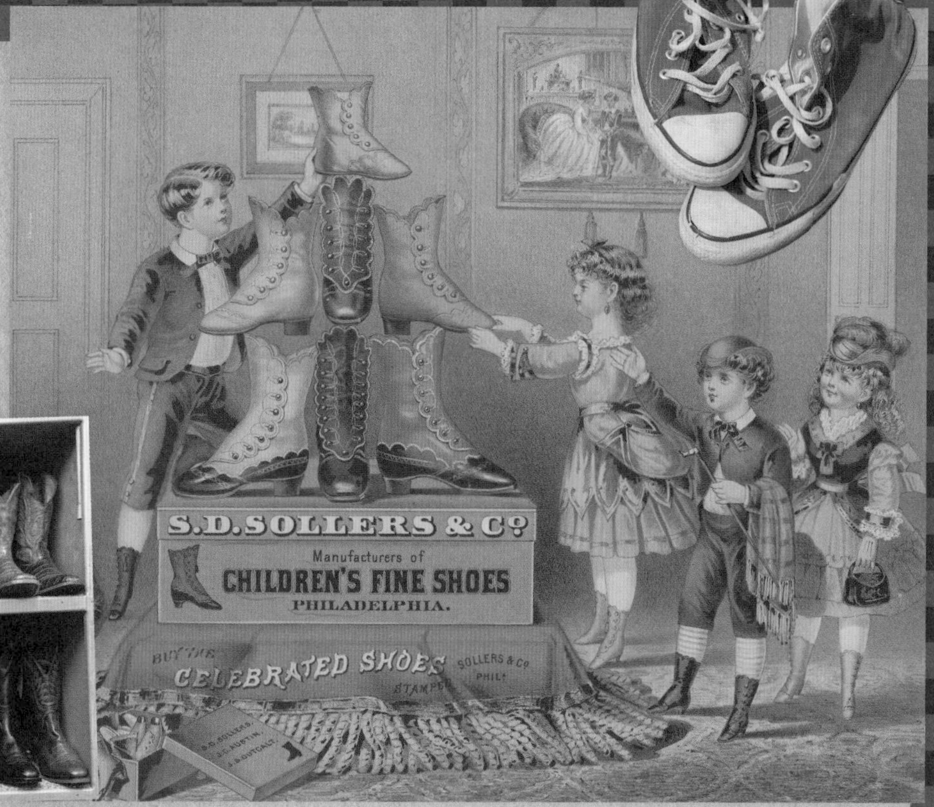

FALL

WINTER

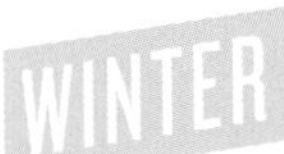

HEAD TO TOE

ACCESSORIZE!

Jewelry, hair ornaments, belts, buckles, scarves: Accessories are found in every culture. They can be symbolic or ornamental, worn as a part of a ritual or for fashion flair—or just to keep warm or hold your pants up!

▶ The Kuba of central Africa are famous for their embroidery. This Kuba belt was made with tiny beads and cowrie shells.

▶ This photo from c. 1910 shows a Wishram bride of the Plateau region in Oregon.

◀ Blue feathers from a kingfisher bird are inlaid into metal in this Chinese hair ornament.

▼ A Hindu bride in Nepal with elaborate accessories

USE THE CLUES TO FILL IN THIS CROSSWORD PUZZLE ABOUT ACCESSORIES.

ACROSS

1 No business suit is complete without one.

5 Keeps you warm in winter, or dresses up an outfit in any season.

7 Goes around your waist.

12 Put these over your peeps when it's sunny out.

13 Keeps hair out of your eyes.

DOWN

2 Decorative fasteners for shirt cuffs.

3 You don't have to be a queen to wear this glittery accessory.

4 Straps to hold up your pants.

6 Hold this in your hand and wave it to keep cool.

8 Donald Duck and Porky Pig both wear this around their necks.

9 Fastens your belt or dresses up your shoes.

10 They keep your hands warm.

11 You can store all your stuff in it, and still look stylish.

HOW BIG IS YOUR WIG?

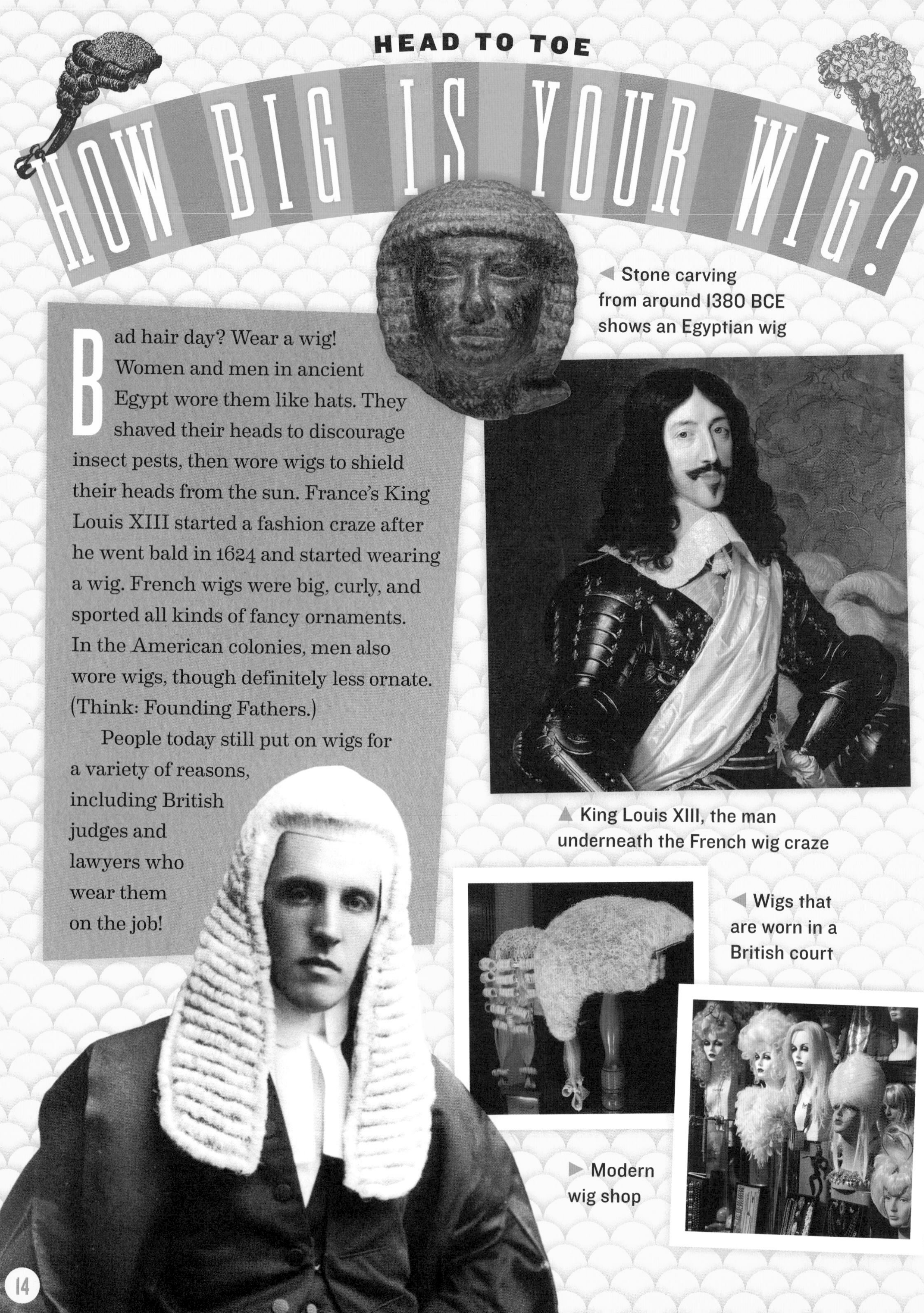

Bad hair day? Wear a wig! Women and men in ancient Egypt wore them like hats. They shaved their heads to discourage insect pests, then wore wigs to shield their heads from the sun. France's King Louis XIII started a fashion craze after he went bald in 1624 and started wearing a wig. French wigs were big, curly, and sported all kinds of fancy ornaments. In the American colonies, men also wore wigs, though definitely less ornate. (Think: Founding Fathers.)

People today still put on wigs for a variety of reasons, including British judges and lawyers who wear them on the job!

◀ Stone carving from around 1380 BCE shows an Egyptian wig

▲ King Louis XIII, the man underneath the French wig craze

◀ Wigs that are worn in a British court

▶ Modern wig shop

DRAW A BIG, CRAZY WIG ON THIS WIG STAND.

HOORAY FOR HATS!

A SIMPLE COTTON BONNET WORN BY A NEW ENGLAND WOMAN IN THE 1800S

PRESIDENT ABRAHAM LINCOLN'S SIGNATURE TOP HAT

A hat protects your head. But it can also let others know how important you are, indicate what role you play in a special ceremony, or make a big fashion statement.

ONLY A MARRIED SOUTH AFRICAN ZULU WOMAN CAN WEAR THIS BEADED HAT.

THE HEIGHT OF FASHION IN THE 1950S

A HAT CAN KEEP YOU WARM . . . AND COOL!

USE THE CLUES TO FILL IN THIS CROSSWORD PUZZLE ABOUT HATS.

ACROSS

1 A Mexican hat with a wide brim and colorful accents.

3 Worn by cattle wranglers, or fans of country music.

5 You don't have to play ball to wear one of these.

7 This round, flat felt cap was made popular by the French.

9 A padded, hard hat worn by football players and fire fighters.

DOWN

2 President Lincoln wore one of these.

4 A hat with three corners, worn by pirates and patriots.

6 This hat shields your face from harmful rays.

8 Construction workers wear this protective hat.

10 A round, red hat with a tassel on top. Used to be the national hat of Turkey.

GO WITH THE FLOW

Clothes made of draped, flowing fabric have been around for centuries.

Indian women started wearing saris about 2,100 years ago—and still wear them today.

In ancient Greece, both men and women wore a simple garment called a chiton.

The Roman toga was heavy and hard to move around in, so only the upper class wore them.

DRAW A CLOTH PATTERN THAT WOULD LOOK GOOD DRAPED.

EVERYDAY DUDS

FASHION DOs AND DON'TS

Some societies have rules about fashion and what people can and cannot wear. These are called sumptuary laws.

▲ From the 1200s through the 1700s in France, only rich people could wear fancy clothes with buckles and lace.

▼ Seventeenth-century Puritans believed that wearing fancy clothes was a sin and forbade it.

IF YOU COULD MAKE RULES ABOUT FASHION, WHAT WOULD THEY BE? WRITE YOUR OWN FASHION DOS AND DON'TS HERE.

DOS	DON'TS

NOW THAT'S A BIG SKIRT!

Hoop skirts—big skirts draped over hoops made of whalebone or wicker—were very popular in the United States in the 1800s. They could be as wide as 18 feet!

DRAW A COMIC SHOWING A PROBLEM YOU MIGHT ENCOUNTER WHILE WEARING A HOOP SKIRT.

RELAX!

Loose gowns were popular leisure wear in colonial America. Nightclothes with pants are called pajamas (pj's for short), named after a loose-flowing style of Persian pants.

GIVE THESE PJ'S SOME PIZZAZZ BY ADDING A PATTERN.

GET DOWN TO BUSINESS

A jacket. Pants. A collared shirt. Maybe a vest. Definitely a tie. These are the ingredients of a modern business suit. (Women might swap in a skirt or lose the tie.) The first business suits appeared in the nineteenth century, when military style fused with men's formal wear.

WHICH WAY WOULD YOU GO: LONG TIE OR BOW? DRAW YOUR NECKWEAR HERE.

ALL-AMERICAN PANTS

The first blue jeans were made by a Bavarian immigrant and merchant named Levi Strauss and his business partner, Jacob Davis. Strauss ran a dry goods business in San Francisco. In 1873, he started selling the sturdy, practical pants to gold miners. Today, people from all walks of life wear them.

USE THE WORD BANK TO FILL IN THE BLANKS IN THIS ARTICLE ABOUT HOW BLUE JEANS ARE MADE.

Most blue jeans are made of ...., a sturdy fabric made of cotton. (Some jeans are made with a .... blend.) Machines spin the .... into yarn, which is .... blue. Early jeans were dyed with a .... called indigo, but today .... indigo is used.

The dyed yarn is .... on a mechanical loom to make .... A worker cuts the fabric into pattern .... These pieces are sewn together by workers on an assembly line using industrial .... machines.

Pockets and belt loops are sewn first. Then the .... are attached to the legs. The leg pieces are sewn together, the waistband is added, and then the .... Buttons or a .... are sewn on. The pants get hemmed, the metal rivets are attached, and the last thing? The company ....

★ ★ ★ ★ WORD BANK ★ ★ ★ ★

belt loops ★ cotton ★ denim ★ dyed ★ fabric ★ label ★ pieces
plant ★ pockets ★ polyester ★ sewing ★ synthetic ★ woven ★ zipper

CUTE KIDS

In the Victorian era (1837–1901), children were often dressed like mini-adults. Clothes for both boys and girls could include lace, ribbons, and frills.

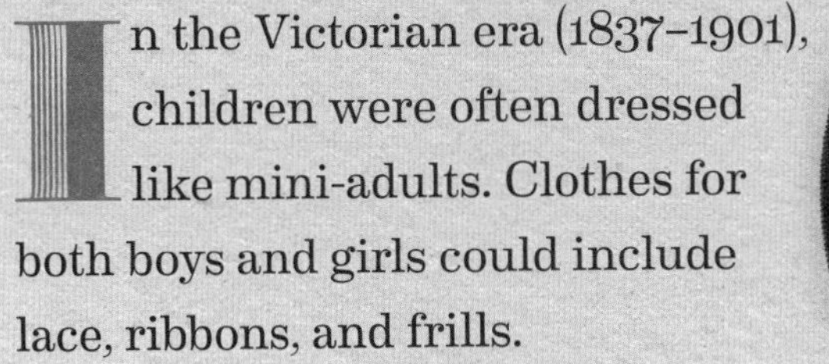

WHAT ARE THESE KIDS THINKING? HOW ABOUT THE DOG? FILL IN THE SPEECH BUBBLES.

SEASIDE STYLE

What could be cooler than going to the ocean on a hot summer day? Well, if you were headed to the beach more than 100 years ago, you'd be wearing a dress if you were a girl or knee-length pants and a shirt if you were a boy. Female bathers didn't start wearing shorter swimsuits until the 1900s, when female athletes ditched long, heavy swimwear so they could compete in swimming events.

USE THE CLUES TO UNSCRAMBLE THE NAMES OF THESE BATHING FASHIONS.

1 Men's bottoms, or what elephants have.

N U K S R T

2 A tiny two-piece.

I N K I I B

3 Worn by surfboarders and paddleboarders.

S B A R R O H O T S D

4 Beach shoes.

P I L F S L O F P

_ _ _ _ - _ _ _ _ _

5 A tank on the top and a bikini on the bottom.

I N K A T N I

6 A long-sleeved athletic shirt that provides protection from the sun and elements.

A H R S U R D A G

7 A scuba diver wears this.

U T I W T E S

8 A more competitive swimmer needs one of these.

W S M I P C A

9 Worn over a swimsuit.

R V C O E P U

_ _ _ _ _ - _ _

10 A long piece of cloth tied around the waist.

A O S R G N

SPECIAL OCCASIONS

THE ROYAL TREATMENT

YOU MIGHT NOT BE A KING OR QUEEN, BUT SOME DAYS YOU MAY FEEL LIKE ONE. DRAW SOMETHING YOU'D WEAR FOR AN IMPORTANT CEREMONY IN YOUR LIFE—LIKE A GRADUATION, WEDDING, OR SPECIAL BIRTHDAY.

◀ This colorful garment was worn by a chief of the African Yoruba tribe in the 1950s.

Kings, queens, and other leaders often wear special garments, headdresses, or crowns. These fashions may signify power or be worn as part of a special ceremony. Royal dress and headwear are often brightly colored and usually made of the finest fabrics, jewels, or other valued materials.

▲ A high-ranking member of the Haida people from Alaska would wear this mask and headdress during a ceremonial feast.

FIRST LADIES OF FASHION

The first First Lady, Martha Washington, wore this painted silk gown in the 1780s.

Mary Todd Lincoln wore this gown in 1861. A very talented African American dressmaker, Elizabeth Keckley, made many of this First Lady's clothes. Keckley had been born enslaved, but eventually bought her own freedom.

This silk satin open-robe style dress was typical of the late 1810s, when Dolley Madison wore it.

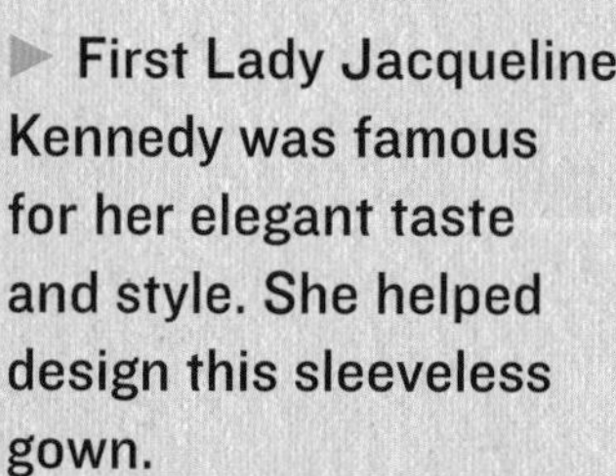

First Lady Jacqueline Kennedy was famous for her elegant taste and style. She helped design this sleeveless gown.

The United States may not have queens, but First Ladies have a history of wearing spectacular gowns on special occasions.

WRITE A FASHION REVIEW OF THESE FIRST LADY GOWNS. DON'T FORGET TO ADD A HEADLINE.

▼ Michelle Obama wore this gown to an inaugural ball in 2013.

SPINNING WORMS

Many gowns are made of silk, a shimmery luxury fabric made from the thread of silkworms. This "worm" is actually a moth larva. Around 5,000 years ago, people in China first figured out how to turn the cocoon threads the larva spins into fabric. For a long time, only royalty was allowed to wear this spun silk.

FOLLOW THE TANGLED LINES TO SEE WHICH SILKWORM'S THREAD WAS USED IN EACH SILK SCARF.

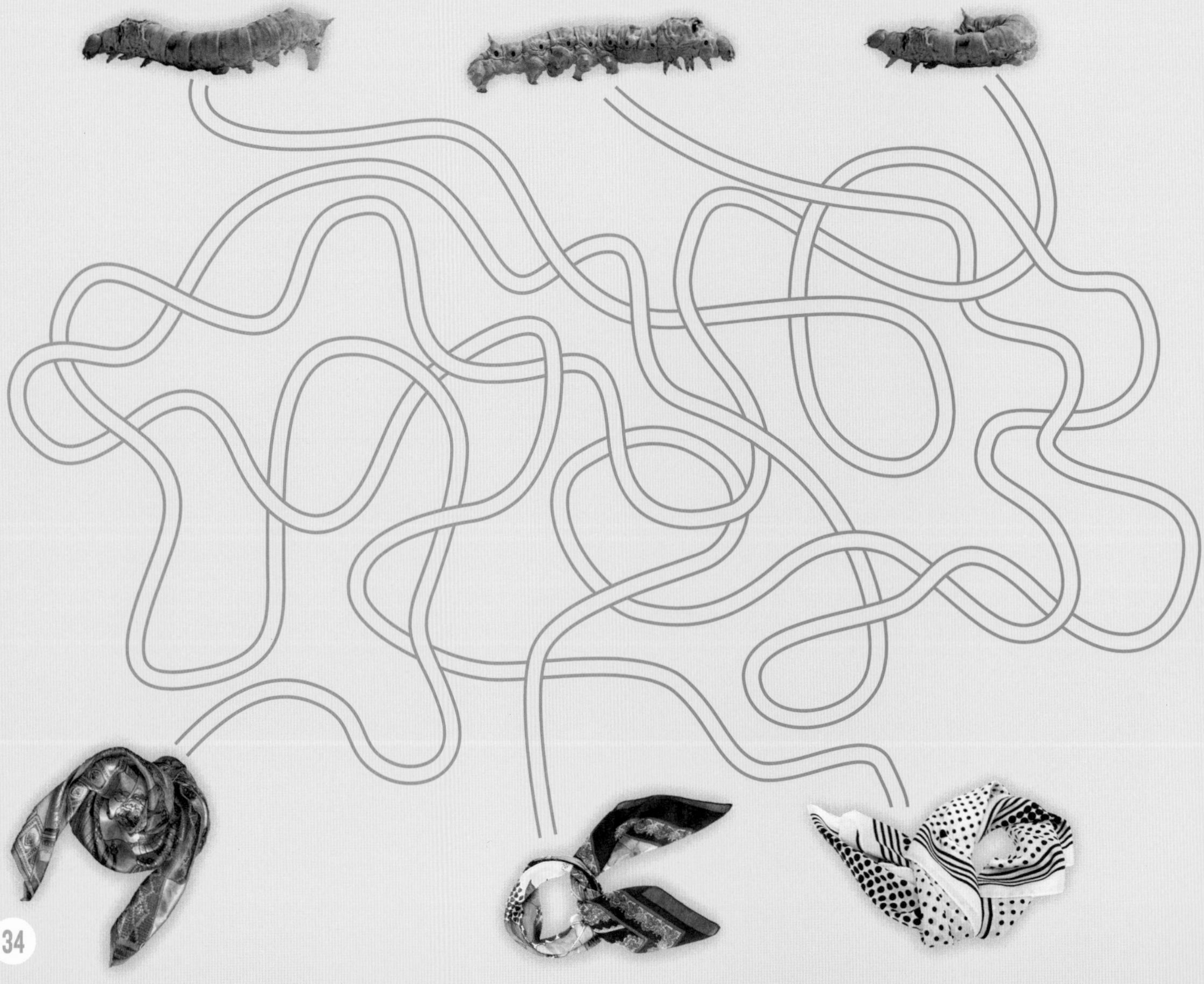

COLOR A KIMONO

Silk is also often used to make kimonos, a style of robe created by the Japanese around the year 794. Kimonos can be dyed beautiful colors or embroidered with designs or scenery. Lavish kimonos may be worn on important occasions such as weddings or festivals.

COLOR IN THIS KIMONO WITH YOUR OWN DESIGN OR PATTERN.

15 CANDLES

A ceremony, a party, and one fantastic gown. These are the ingredients of the Mexican tradition *quinceañera*, a special celebration that takes place when a girl turns fifteen years old.

WHAT WOULD YOU WEAR TO CELEBRATE YOUR FIFTEENTH BIRTHDAY? A FANCY GOWN? A TUX? JEANS AND A T-SHIRT? DRAW YOUR DREAM PARTY OUTFIT HERE.

PLAID ABOUT YOU

The plaid pattern on a kilt is called a tartan. The first Scottish kilts appeared in the sixteenth century. They were worn by men on formal occasions—and even into battle, as recently as World War II.

ADD A TARTAN PATTERN TO THIS KILT USING YOUR FAVORITE COLORS.

SPECIAL OCCASIONS

SHINING ARMOR

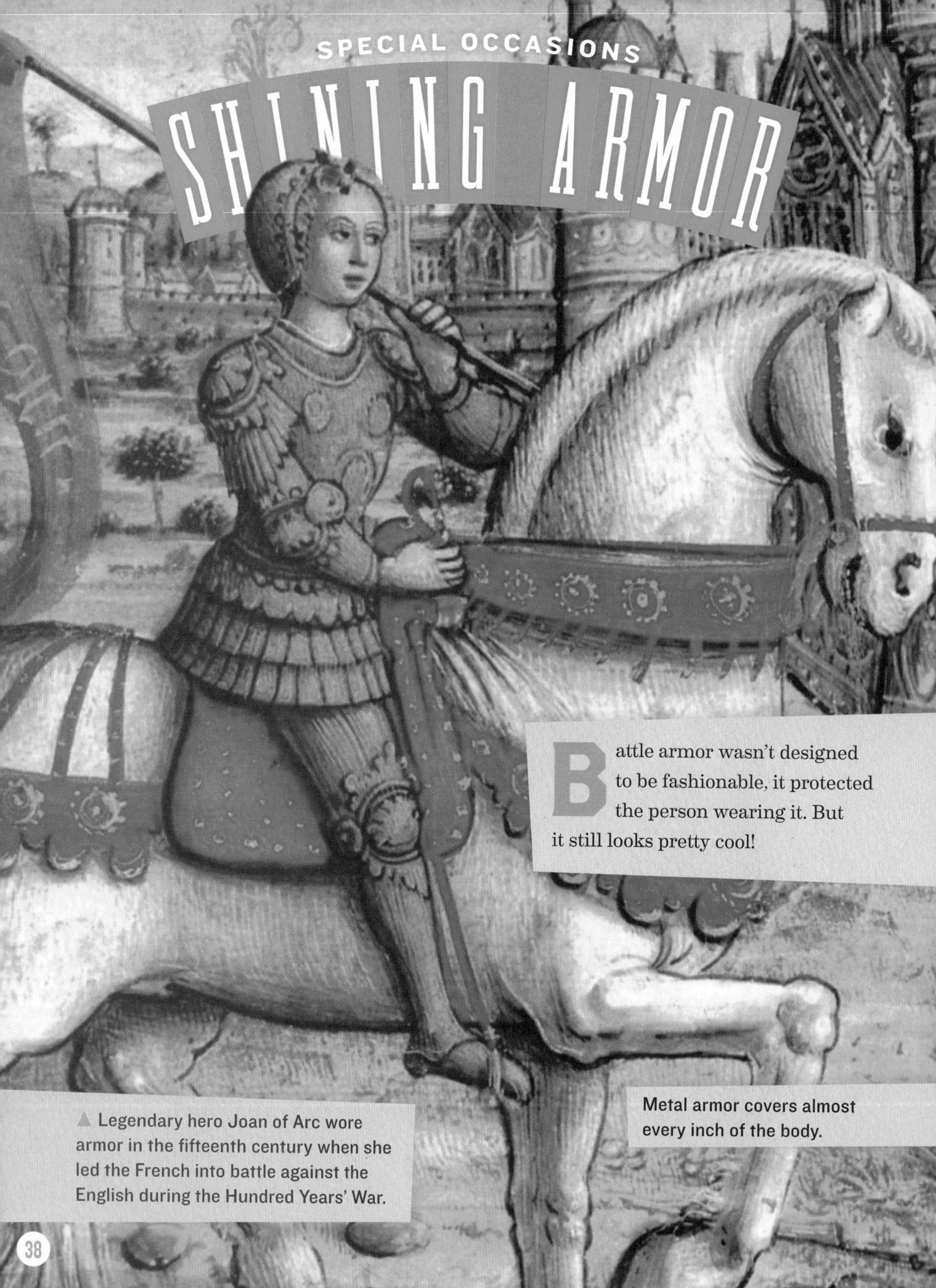

Battle armor wasn't designed to be fashionable, it protected the person wearing it. But it still looks pretty cool!

▲ Legendary hero Joan of Arc wore armor in the fifteenth century when she led the French into battle against the English during the Hundred Years' War.

Metal armor covers almost every inch of the body.

WHAT ARE THESE KNIGHTS SAYING? ADD DIALOGUE.

MAKING A STATEMENT

WHEEL OF FASHION

To turn plant fibers or wool into fabric, first you have to spin it into thread. During the American Revolution, spinning became a political act. Women patriots took part in the "homespun movement" to make their own fabric, instead of buying cloth from the British.

The spinning wheel is believed to have been invented in India, somewhere between the year 500 and 1,000. Around the world, spinning was done by hand using a spindle or a spinning wheel, until mechanical spinning was invented in the eighteenth century. Women in rural areas continued to use spinning wheels into the twentieth century.

WHAT MIGHT THESE WOMEN BE SPINNING? DRAW THE END PRODUCT THAT COMES FROM THEIR THREAD.

MAKING A STATEMENT

BRING ON THE BLOOMERS!

Imagine running, climbing, or riding a bicycle in a long, heavy skirt or dress. That's what you'd be doing if you were an American woman in the nineteenth century (if you even did such things!). In the 1850s, some bold women, such as women's rights champion and newspaper publisher Amelia Bloomer, bravely started wearing trouser outfits. These "bloomers" didn't catch on at first, but when bicycles became popular, shorter skirts and eventually pants did, too.

In order to ride bicycles, women needed clothing that wouldn't get stuck in the bike. This helped spark dress reform.

CREATE A CONVINCING AD FOR THAT WONDERFUL NEW TREND IN WOMEN'S CLOTHING: BLOOMERS!

MAKING A STATEMENT

AFRICAN STYLE

During the late twentieth century, some clothing in the United States reflected a new appreciation for heritage and identity. Some African American men wore dashikis, colorful shirts originally from West Africa. Kente cloth, an intricately woven cloth native to Ghana, also became popular.

◄ **An Asanti weaver from Ghana weaves a colorful strip of kente cloth.**

KENTE CLOTH COLORS AND PATTERNS HAVE DIFFERENT MEANINGS. DESIGN A CLOTH PATTERN THAT REFLECTS YOUR HERITAGE. LABEL THE COLORS AND PATTERNS WITH THEIR MEANINGS.

Dashikis often contain symbols and designs, like these hearts and flowers.

THE ROARING 20S

American women won the right to vote in 1920. Some of them expressed their new freedom through fashion. These "flappers" cut their hair short and went short on dresses and skirts as well.

THE WAY FLAPPERS SPOKE WAS AS NEW AND FREE AS THEIR FASHIONS. MATCH EACH OF THE 1920S SLANG EXPRESSIONS TO ITS MEANING.

1. the bee's knees
2. cheaters
3. beat it
4. big cheese
5. dolled up
6. gams
7. owl
8. tomato
9. wet blanket
10. sap

A. someone who stays up late
B. someone who is no fun
C. someone important
D. eyeglasses
E. dressed up
F. a fool
G. something awesome
H. get lost
I. legs
J. a woman

THE LOOK

1930s GLAM

In the 1930s, some women copied the glamorous looks of Hollywood film stars. Cosmetics gave actresses a dramatic look onscreen, and their fans used various powders and other makeup to do the same.

SINCE ANCIENT TIMES IN EGYPT, FASHIONABLE WOMEN AND MEN HAVE USED MAKEUP. CIRCLE THE WORDS ABOUT COSMETICS HIDDEN IN THIS PUZZLE. LOOK UP, DOWN, BACKWARD, AND DIAGONALLY.

B E A B R O N Z E R U R
B L U E L P O L I S H E
T I I Y P U R P L E F D
U P L E Y E S H A D O W
M G O L V I E H S T A O
R L L I P L I N E R L P
F O U N D A T I O N O I
O S R E L A E C N O C N
K S A R A C S A M L O K
V E L L I P S T I C K Y

★ ★ ★ ★ ★ ★ ★ ★ WORD BANK ★ ★ ★ ★ ★ ★ ★ ★

blue ★ blush ★ bronzer ★ concealer ★ eyeliner ★ eye shadow ★ foundation
lip gloss ★ lip liner ★ lipstick ★ mascara ★ pink ★ polish ★ powder ★ purple

THE FIGHTING 40S

World War II (1939–1945) had a big impact on women's fashions in the 1940s. "Victory Suits" had shorter skirts, thanks to a fabric shortage, and jackets with shoulder pads, inspired by military uniforms. With men off fighting, some women on the home front worked in jobs that required pants or uniforms.

DESIGN AN OUTFIT FOR YOURSELF THAT GOES WITH EACH OF THESE WORLD WAR II SCENARIOS.

HANDS-ON FACTORY WORK

FABRIC SHORTAGE

THE FUN 50S

After World War II ended, Americans celebrated happier times with fun fashion trends. Girls wore circle-shaped skirts decorated with poodles, called—what else?—poodle skirts! And both men and women wore low-heeled, white leather shoes with a black saddle-shaped panel.

DRAW AN ANIMAL THEME ON THE CIRCLE SKIRT AND GIVE THE SADDLE SHOES A NEW, HIP COLOR.

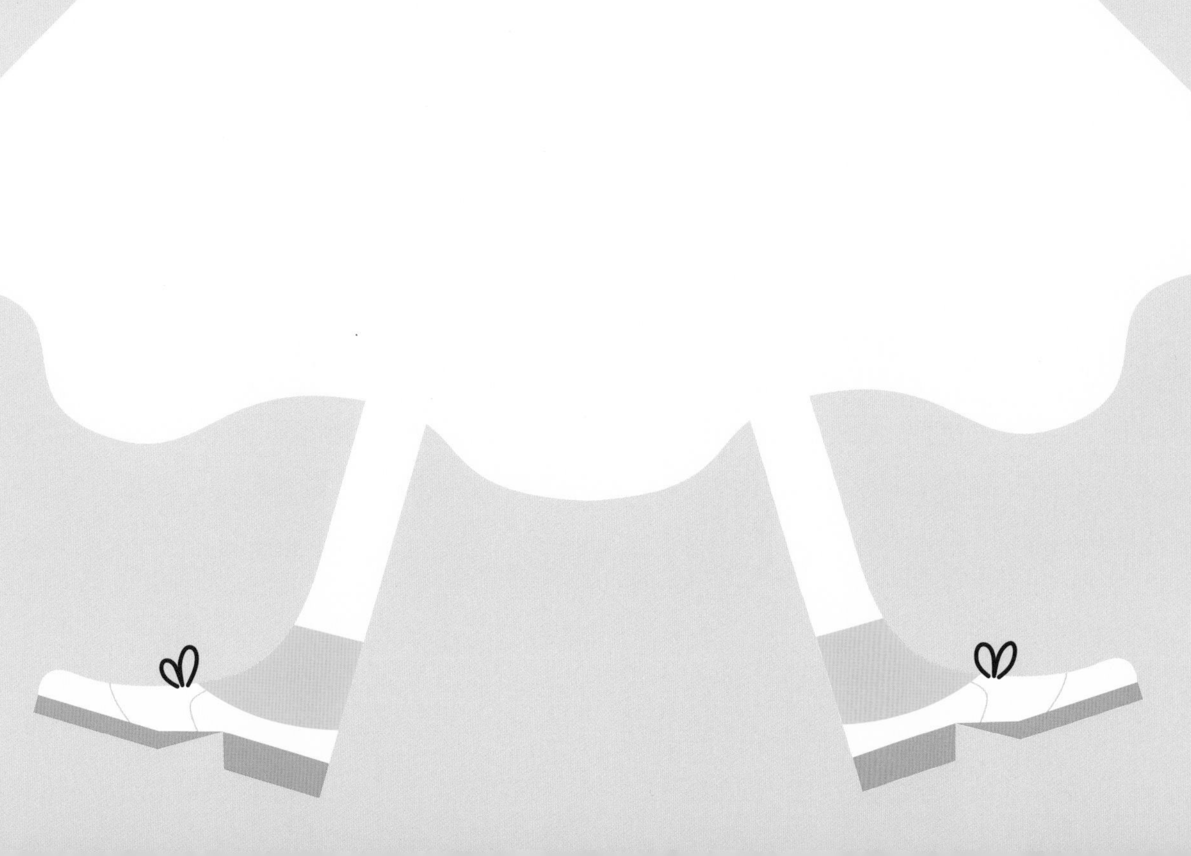

THE LOOK

PEACE, LOVE, AND 60s FASHION

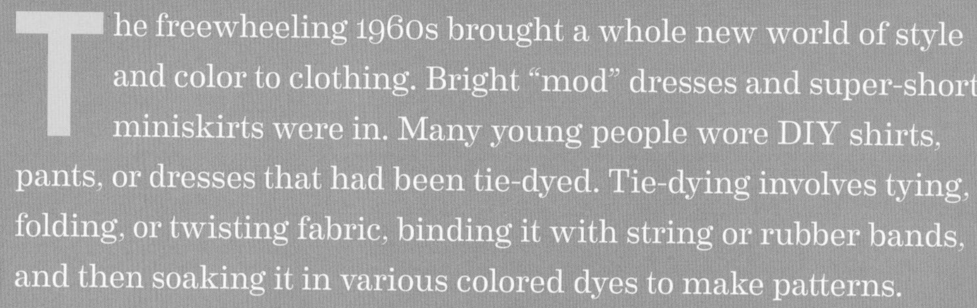

The freewheeling 1960s brought a whole new world of style and color to clothing. Bright "mod" dresses and super-short miniskirts were in. Many young people wore DIY shirts, pants, or dresses that had been tie-dyed. Tie-dying involves tying, folding, or twisting fabric, binding it with string or rubber bands, and then soaking it in various colored dyes to make patterns.

TIE-DYE THIS T-SHIRT BY COLORING IN A PATTERN.

70s FASHION FLUBS

Many people would say that the 1970s were a low point in contemporary western fashion: wide-legged, bell-bottom pants. Crazy-high platform shoes. The big-collared, loud-colored, polyester leisure suit.

WHAT CURRENT FASHION WOULD YOU NOMINATE FOR THE BAD FASHION HALL OF FAME? DRAW AND LABEL YOUR ANSWER AS TO WHY.

THE BIG-HAIR 80S

People now make fun of 1980s fashions, too. Musicians in "hair metal" bands inspired men and women to sport big, wavy hairstyles. Guys wore parachute pants made of nylon, and women wore leg warmers over their acid-washed jeans. Preppies—kids who went to expensive private or "prep" schools—created their own influential styles. Girls wore pastel sweaters with pearls, and guys wore polo shirts or draped sweaters around their shoulders.

DO YOU SPEAK 80S? SEE IF YOU CAN FIGURE OUT WHAT THESE SLANG WORDS FROM THE 1980S MEAN. CIRCLE YOUR ANSWER.

1	sweet	A a nice person	B something that is very good
2	wigging	A freaking out	B wearing a wig
3	book	A to leave in a hurry	B to go to the library
4	kicks	A fun times	B shoes
5	warped	A something that doesn't fit	B something disturbing
6	zeek	A a super geek	B stylish
7	space cadet	A an astronaut	B someone who is not focused
8	shred	A to give an amazing performance	B to get upset
9	icy	A awesome	B an unfriendly person
10	grindage	A loud music	B food

THE MUSICAL 90S

Some of the most memorable fashions of the 1990s were influenced by music. Fans of grunge music popularized the affordable combo of plaid flannel shirts and jeans. Hip-hop music sparked a trend toward branded gear, baggy clothes, and bold colors.

OVER THE DECADES, MUSIC HAS INFLUENCED FASHION. MATCH THE MUSIC STYLE ON THE LEFT TO THE ITEM OF CLOTHING ON THE RIGHT THAT ONE OF ITS FANS MIGHT HAVE WORN.

1. heavy metal
2. grunge
3. The Beatles
4. punk
5. hip-hop
6. disco

A. miniskirt
B. baggy jeans
C. jacket with safety pins
D. plaid flannel shirt
E. leather vest (or spiked wristband)
F. glittery shirt

SCHOOL OF FASHION

It's not clear when kids first donned school uniforms. Historians know that children attending charity schools in England in the 1600s had to wear long blue robes. Children in many countries around the world, including most British kids, still wear uniforms. In the United States, uniforms are not the rule in most public schools, though many private schools require them.

WOULD YOU WANT TO WEAR A SCHOOL UNIFORM? OR DO YOU WEAR ONE ALREADY? MAKE A PROS AND CONS LIST ABOUT REQUIRING THEM.

PROS	CONS

GAME TIME!

The first Olympic Games were held in Greece in the eighth century BCE. And you know what those competing in the games wore? Nothing! The kind of sports uniforms that we know today—with different colors or symbols for each team—didn't appear until the 1700s.

GET YOUR SPORTS GEAR TOGETHER. LOOK UP, DOWN, ACROSS, BACKWARD, AND DIAGONALLY FOR THE WORDS FROM THE WORD BANK.

D	R	A	U	G	H	T	U	O	M	M	K	A
G	L	O	V	E	S	F	R	T	J	I	N	T
I	L	S	H	D	R	A	T	O	E	L	E	R
A	R	H	T	E	S	C	K	A	R	A	E	A
T	G	O	G	G	L	E	S	E	J	U	P	C
J	E	R	S	E	Y	M	D	O	T	A	A	K
A	I	T	C	S	T	A	E	L	C	C	D	S
H	I	S	E	O	H	S	Y	T	O	G	S	U
S	E	T	A	K	S	K	E	I	K	O	G	I
T	S	H	I	R	T	A	G	O	A	R	D	T

WORD BANK

cap ★ cleats ★ face mask ★ gloves ★ goggles ★ helmet ★ jersey ★ keikogi
knee pads ★ leotard ★ mouth guard ★ shoes ★ shorts ★ skates ★ T-shirt ★ tracksuit

FROM BATTLEFIELD TO RUNWAY

Both men and women have found fashion inspiration in military uniforms. During the Napoleonic Wars in the 1800s, men's jackets copied the fancy trim of military jackets. World War II soldiers made cargo pants popular, and camouflage became a fashion trend after the Vietnam War.

◀ During World War II, some women made wedding gowns from their fiancé's parachute.

▶ Bomber jackets, worn by World War II air force servicemen, also became popular.

MILITARY CAMOUFLAGE IS DESIGNED TO KEEP THE WEARER FROM BEING SEEN. BUT AS FASHION, CAMOUFLAGE MAKES A STATEMENT. ADD A CAMO PATTERN TO THIS JACKET AND DRAW IN A BACKGROUND SHOWING WHERE YOU MIGHT WEAR IT.

ANIMAL FASHIONS

THE WELL-DRESSED PET

Since the nineteenth-century Victorian era, some people have thought the idea of putting cats and dogs in costumes was a good one. Today, Americans spend more than $350 million on Halloween costumes for their furry friends.

SHOULD YOU DRESS YOUR PETS?

	1	2	3	4	5
YES					
NO					

DO YOU BELIEVE IN DRESSING UP PETS IN COSTUMES AND CUTE CLOTHES? SURVEY YOUR FRIENDS AND FAMILY MEMBERS. CHART THE RESULTS IN A BAR GRAPH. COLOR IN ONE SQUARE FOR EACH ANSWER YOU GET.

6 7 8 9 10 11

FUTURE FABULOUS

HIGH-TECH FASHION

WHAT DO YOU THINK THE FASHION OF THE FUTURE WILL LOOK LIKE? DRAW YOUR IDEAS HERE.

In the twenty-first century, fashion has been lighting up the runway—literally. Some designers integrate technology into their designs. Dresses glow with LED lights. A solar-powered bikini can charge your cell phone. Shimmery dresses change color when somebody looks at them. Right now, it looks like technology is the future of fashion!

ANSWER KEY

PAGES 4-5

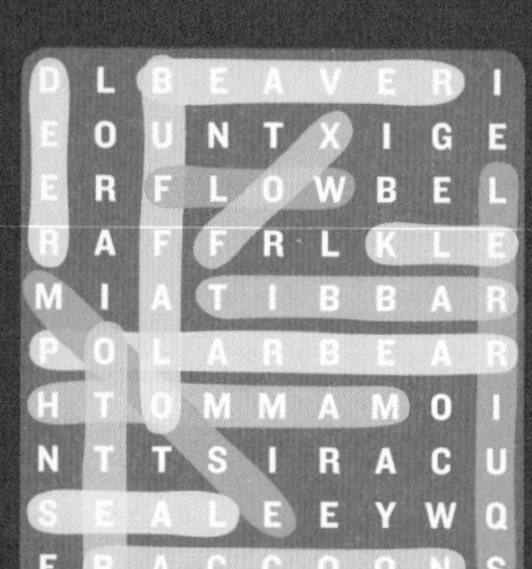

PAGES 6-7

PAGES 8-9

1. I
2. F
3. H
4. G
5. E
6. D
7. C
8. A
9. B

PAGES 12-13

PAGES 16-17

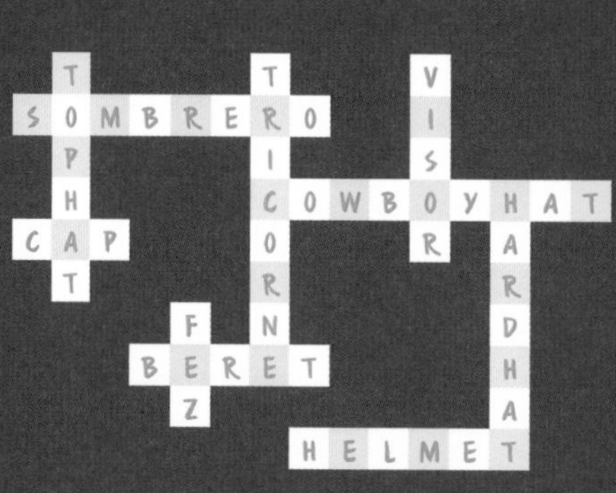

PAGE 25

Most blue jeans are made of DENIM, a sturdy fabric made of cotton. (Some jeans are made with a POLYESTER blend.) Machines spin the COTTON into yarn, which is DYED blue. Early jeans were dyed with a PLANT called indigo, but today SYNTHETIC indigo is used.

The dyed yarn is WOVEN on a mechanical loom to make FABRIC. A worker cuts the fabric into pattern PIECES. These pieces are sewn together by workers on an assembly line using industrial SEWING machines.

Pockets and belt loops are sewn first. Then the POCKETS are attached to the legs. The leg pieces are sewn together, the waistband is added, and then the BELT LOOPS. Buttons or a ZIPPER are sewn on. The pants get hemmed, the metal rivets are attached, and the last thing? The company LABEL.

PAGES 28-29

1. Trunks
2. Bikini
3. Boardshorts
4. Flip-flops
5. Tankini
6. Rash guard
7. Wet suit
8. Swim cap
9. Cover-up
10. Sarong

PAGE 34

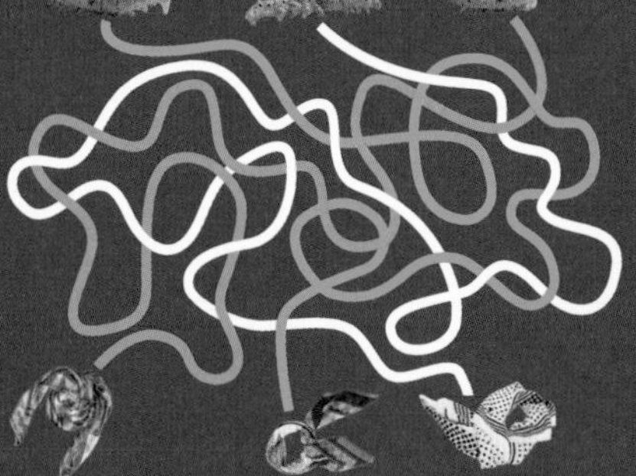

PAGE 46

1. G
2. D
3. H
4. C
5. E
6. I
7. A
8. J
9. B
10. F

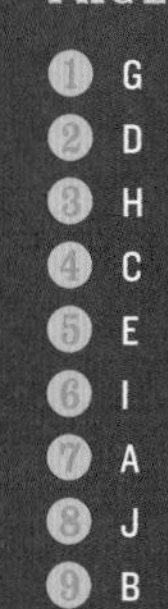

PAGE 47

PAGE 52

1. B
2. A
3. A
4. B
5. B
6. A
7. B
8. A
9. A
10. B

PAGE 53

1. E
2. D
3. A
4. C
5. B
6. F

PAGES 56-57

D R A U G H T U O M M K A
G L O V E S F R T J I N T
I L S H D R A T O E L E R
A R H T E S C K A R A E A
T G O G G L E S E J U P C
J E R S E Y M D O T A A K
A I T C S T A E L C C D S
H I S E O H S Y T O G S U
S E T A K S K E I K O G I
T S H I R T A G O A R D T